LORD TEACH ME
HOW TO PRAY

10 Petitions That Strengthen Your
Relationship with God 2nd Edition

Rodney Perry
Diane Smith
Mark C. Overton

ISBN: 978-1-64314-776-5 (Paperback)
        978-1-64314-777-2 (E-book)

AuthorsPress
California, USA
www.authorspress.com

I dedicate this book to my loving and supportive wife, Lynn. Thank you for allowing me the time to do ministry and making the sacrifices needed to support me in ministry. I dedicate this book to you, as you have given much time in prayer for our family, marriage, and children.

—Rodney Perry

To Terry, Randy, and Terrence: I hope this book inspires you

—Diane Smith

Glory to God for giving Rod, my best friend, this vision and stretching our faith to put this vision into action. I dedicate this second edition of Lord Teach Me How to Pray to my mother, Gloria McGriff, who emboldened our education and trained us siblings up in the church and to my wife, Margarita Overton, whose joy for reading books encourages me to write and be a blessing to others.

—Mark C. Overton

…one of His disciples said to Him, "Lord, teach us to pray…"

—Luke 11:1

Contacting God: When you look at the woman with the issue of blood (Mark 5: 24-34), she just wanted to touch the hem of Jesus garment. She felt touching Jesus would heal her and be the answer to her problems. She had this problem for 12 years. How long have we been dealing with the same problem? The old woman did just that. What was amazing is that even though Jesus was touched by a lot of people because he was walking amongst a crowd of people, he felt her touch was different. In fact, Jesus said power left him after she touched his hem. What that tells you is that the woman with the issue of blood made contact, where others in the crowd did not make contact. That lady was expecting God to do something for us. When it comes to prayer, many of us pray; but are you making contact. This book will teach you how to contact Jesus via your prayer life. To contact a person, there must be an agreement of the minds on a situation.

Are you ready to contact Jesus? After reading this book, you will create an intimate relationship with God that will birth your dreams and goals from the invisible to the visible. Let's create some intimacy with Our God.

We look upon prayer simply as a means of getting things for ourselves, but the biblical purpose of prayer is that we may get to know God Himself.

"Ask, and you will receive…" (John 16:24). Yet a child exhibits a magnificent boldness to ask! Our Lord said, "…unless you…become as little children…" (Matthew 18:3). Ask and God will do. Give Jesus Christ the opportunity and the room to work.

The problem is that no one will ever do this until he is at his wits' end. When a person is at his wits' end, it no longer seems to be a cowardly thing to pray; in fact, it is the only way he can get in touch with the truth and the reality of God Himself. Be yourself before God and present Him with your problems—the very things that have brought you to your wits' end. But if you think you are self-sufficient; you do not need to ask God for anything.

To say that "prayer changes things" is not as close to the truth as saying, "Prayer changes me and then I change things." God has established things so that prayer, based on redemption, changes the way a person looks at things. Prayer is not a matter of changing things externally, but one of working miracles in a person's inner nature.

—OSWALD CHAMBERS

Contents

Preface

THE BIBLE SAYS THAT God wants you to talk with him now and have a personal relationship with him. But how do you do that? Communication with God is called prayer. The word "pray" which Jesus uses throughout the New Testament is the most simple and basic of all the words for prayer, and it means to "wish forward" or "desire onward." As Dr. Tony Evans, a Christian pastor, speaker, author, and a widely-syndicated U.S. radio and television broadcaster, stated, "Prayer is the vehicle that connects the natural with the supernatural".

God wants to hear the desires of your heart now. And like communicating and giving fully undivided attention with your spouse, you can instantly strengthen your relationship with Christ by conversing often with him through prayer.

Normally we pray only when we need God's help with a particular issue. Surveys show more than 90% of America pray daily. For example, you may call out to him to help you when a spouse has a surgery or a family member loses a job. While requests are surely heard, his deepest desire is to continuously increase communion with you through prayer.

In his book, *Let's Talk,* Bill Crowder, Associate Bible Teacher and Director of Ministry Content for RBC Ministries, assures us, "Prayer is not something we say to God; it is something we do together *with* our God! Bill Crowder, who is also a contributor to

Our Daily Bread, says "The Godhead joins us in our prayers and responds to our prayers:

Because the Father, in compassion, sees and hears,

Because the Son is constantly interceding for us at the Father's side, and,

Because the Holy Spirit is interpreting our prayers in order to bring our hearts in line with God's good purpose for us."

The LORD's Prayer, one of the best loved and most spoken prayers on the planet, is important to you, as a Christian, because it is what Jesus gave to his disciples as a startling form of prayer when they asked him to teach them HOW to pray—about God and your needs.

As you set aside a specific time to pray today, the Lord's Prayer will inspire you to quickly discover and increase its pattern of prayer. Thus, you may first pray: "LORD, I ask for your help and your divine power to assist me in faithfully and consistently teaching me how to pray with more focus over the next 10 days and every day."

Introduction

Elevate Your Prayer Level from Religion to Relationship

THE MAIN WAY OF developing a relationship with God is though prayer. If you want to feel loved and connected to your partner in a healthy relationship, good communication is a key part of any relationship; it can increase trust and strengthen the bond between you. Similarly, the biblical purpose of prayer is to get to know him; the Bible says he wants you to talk and have a personal relationship with him. He also wants to hear the free-flowing, outpouring desires of your heart, and the main way in which you hear him is accessing his word.

God longs for you to talk to him about what is on your heart. You don't need to hold back or censor what you talk to him about or try to come across as something you are not. He already knows everything about you; he wants to hear it from you and to talk it through with you. Be yourself with God when you pray—not the way you think you should be. God would never give up on those who love him, and that compassion gives you hope.

And you can pray in all circumstances. Pray every way you know how, and for everyone you know. If you are hurting or in trouble, pray. If you are feeling great or happy, sing songs of praise. If you are sick, call the elders … and pray. If you have sinned, confess your sins and pray for healing and restoration. When things are kept hidden in the dark, they can have a destructive power. But when we bring them out into the light, we are set free. Pray to find one person you can trust and with whom you can be honest, vulnerable, and empty yourself. Prayer is powerful and effective.

You also have no limit to the times, places and different ways in which you can pray. Muslims pray in the direction of the Middle East; Bodybuilders go to "Muscle Mass" every Sunday to pray. Pray always; without ceasing; at all times; three or seven times a day; morning, noon, evening; at midnight; in the assembly or congregation; your closet; vehicle, or in any place you can draw near to God. You can also pray while standing up or walking around; some people kneel when they pray because they're trying to save their soles. God hears and sees you, the Father has compassion for you, and the Holy Spirit can intercede for you.

And millions of people, ranging from devout believers to worldly folk pray each day. Christians pray The Lord's Prayer 95% of the time. The Lord's Prayer is a prayer that Jesus taught his disciples in Matthew 6:9-13 and Luke 11:2-4. Do you know what you're praying? Do you comprehend The LORD's Prayer? Many people misunderstand the LORD's Prayer to be a prayer you're supposed to recite word for word. Some people treat the LORD's Prayer as a magic formula, as if the words themselves have some specific power or influence with God. For many when it's recited or memorized, they rehearse only words, traditions or a routine. For this reason, prayer suddenly becomes religion versus relationship. But the Bible teaches the opposite. He is far more interested in your hearts when you pray than he is in your words. In prayer, pour out your heart to him instead of simply reciting memorized words to him. Similarly, some people recite the pledge of allegiance, but to a person in the military, the pledge represents a way of life and promotes a sign of honor and respect. Likewise, parents may teach kids to recount The LORD's Prayer like echoing the alphabets. They're so happy when their children learn The LORD's Prayer. And shameful, too often, we keep our children at the "LORD teach us to pray" level. And we never teach them relationship improvement with God, because we were never taught.

Understand the LORD's Prayer as an example, a pattern, of how to pray. It gives you the "ingredients" that should go into prayer. To better understand the LORD's Prayer, its subtitle, "10 Petitions That Strengthen Your Relationship with God" consists of two parts—glorifying God and sustaining your Needs. The first five chapters, from "Our Father" to "Thy will be done on earth as it is in heaven," is about God; the second five chapters, from "Give us today our daily bread" to "Amen" is about our needs. These petitions help you know what you're praying for. Prayer is a dialogue versus a monologue, and God speaks to you as you pray. We believe Jesus provided his disciples (and us) a repeatable template on how to pray, to keep prayer in focus, and lead you into relationship.

Here is how it is broken down: "Our Father in heaven" teaches you whom to address your prayers to—the Father. "Hallowed be your name" tells you to worship and praise him for who he is. The phrase "your kingdom come, your will be done on earth as it is in heaven" reminds you to pray for his plan in your life and the world. You pray for his will to be done instead of your desires. In addition, you're encouraged to ask him for things you need in "give us today our daily bread." "Forgive us our debts, as we also have forgiven our debtors" harkens you to confess your sins to him and to turn from them, and to also forgive others as he has forgiven you. The conclusion of the Lord's Prayer, "And lead us not into temptation, but deliver us from the evil one" is a plea for help in achieving victory over sin, and a request for protection from the attacks of the devil. Have you ever felt like you were in the depths of despair? Have you felt like 'the bottom' has fallen out of [your] life? Prayers lay the track which God's power can come. This devotional's simple purpose is to instantly offer you the proper method and new posture on how to pray and discover insight on Jesus' remarkable words. In Matthew 6, when the disciples asked Jesus to teach them how to pray, they instantly repeated what he said. Friend, you can pray like Jesus prayed and use the same time-tested, quotable, repeatable, portable prayer method, keeping your prayer in focus– a no-brainer. It gives you a great outline for making contact with him.

So, again, the Lord's Prayer is not a prayer you memorize and recite back to God. Use it as an example of how you should pray. Is there anything wrong with memorizing the Lord's Prayer? Of course not! Is there anything wrong with praying the Lord's Prayer back to him? Nope, especially when your heart is in it and you truly mean the words you say. He's far more interested in you communicating with him and speaking from your heart than in the specific words you use.

It's encouraging to know that God hears you regardless of the language, length or logic of your prayers. Many of us can't pray for 5 minutes nor amazingly 1 hour because our prayer gets boring and repetitive. Roman 8:26 tells us, "We do not know what to pray for as we ought." And the same passage adds "the Spirit himself intercedes for us with groaning too deep for words." We lack focus and start wondering and thinking about everything else. Like a laser beam cutting through steel, you can also focus your prayer— from recite to ripe; its impact can suddenly cut every stronghold in your life, or cut-up the enemy's plan. A sight for sore eyes, many folk fall asleep, increase attention deficit disorder, and forget what it is they prayed.

Abide with me to focus your prayer now, you may also compare the ACTS method as a miracle prayer strategy:

Adoration (adoring God for who he is),

Confession (being or getting right with him)

Thanksgiving (taking time to show your thankfulness for what he has done for you)

Supplication (presenting your requests to the LORD).

Well, enough of your authentic prayer being a mess—it's not a show, act or pretense; it's time to instantly organize it and talk with your heavenly Father about what's on your mind now. What if you and I were having a conversation and you continued to change subjects, forget your thoughts, or fall asleep? Would we have a productive talk? If our chat is disrupted and you asked for something, the challenge is to stay focused to receive your request. Accordingly, you may not get what you asked for.

Also, when Jesus said the Spirit already knows what you want to pray for, it does not give you a way out of not having to pray—not the case at all. It means God already amazingly knows your thoughts, but it doesn't relieve you from praying. For example, a parent of a child will sometimes know what their son or daughter needs. And they will get the child to ask nicely for it first with no strings attached. So by asking him for things in prayer, it teaches us to respect him and to see him as our heavenly Father.

Prayer is for you and not for God. He is fine and he has everything you need; but you need to understand that he wants to work through you and others to suddenly give you your exclusive desires and needs. Therefore, prayer helps you keep the things and acts of God a priority. He will immediately make your things a priority once you make the things of his a priority. Matthew 6:33 says, "But put God's kingdom first. Do what he wants you to do. Then all those things will also be given to you." Prayer is one of the ways you can communicate with him. Anytime spent with God our Father is important. Trust!

Prayer is a way you can communicate with God. Unfortunately many people are uncomfortable or intimidated with prayer. We recommend you use the Lord's Prayer, a template Jesus used when the disciples asked him how to pray versus what to pray. They didn't walk away saying, "Hey, I have this prayer thing figured out." And if they needed prayer guidance, why should we be embarrassed or afraid to pray or communicate with him? The problem is that we never learned how to pray.

Regardless of the prayer model or "standard" of prayer (world, church, etc.), God desires a sincere heart. The bonus goal of praying isn't to sound super spiritual, but to connect at the deepest possible place with him. So whenever you come to the Father, he will look at your heart and judge the sincerity in which you came. Never ever be afraid to come to him in prayer; he knows all, and there aren't any secrets.

Satan wants you to fear coming to God in prayer or make you feel like God is unconcerned with anything you have to say. He also wants you to believe that God does not exist and therefore ironclad prayer is unneeded—a lie from the pits of hell. His basic

methods are guilt and inferiority, shame and doubt—to make you
feel he is not interested in anything you have to say. Satan will do
anything to keep you from having a strong relationship with God.
Be enthralled always, and remember that God loves you and desires
an intimate relationship with you. Master, teach us to pray:

Our Father
Who Art in Heaven
Hallow Be Thy Name
Thy Kingdom Come
Thy Will Be Done on Earth As it is in Heaven
Give Us This Day Our Daily Bread
Forgive us for our Debts, as we also have forgiven our Debtor
And Lead Us Not into Temptation but Deliver Us from Evil
For Thine is the Kingdom, the Power and the Glory For ever
Amen

No beating around the bush, *LORD Teach Me How to Pray*
motivates you to see your prayer time as special, life-changing and
memorable. It'll strengthen your faith and spiritually catapult you
today. For God is a Spirit and we must worship him in spirit and
truth now.

Glorifying God

Chapter 1

Our Father

T HIS IS HOW YOU should pray. Who are you praying to? Notice that Jesus told the disciples to start with "Our Father." You're not praying to the porcelain altar. And you can make contact with him by saying, "Hi God. It's me" and then pray your heart and reveal yourself.

When you think of the word *father*, what word and feelings come to mind? Merriam-Webster's definition of 'father'; is: "a male parent, a man who is thought of as being like a father, a person who was in someone's family in past times." For all intents and purposes, your definition may be different. It may depend on whether you had a father or not, or what kind of father he was.

If your father is/was loving, some of the words you may use would be: loving, warm, compassionate, safe, secure, trustworthy, accepting, firm. If you've never had a father in your life, your feelings could be unworthiness, abandonment, emptiness, insecurity, poor self-esteem, or a list of other negative emotions. If your father is/ was a strict disciplinarian, there are other feelings such as harshness, pain, fear, rejection, unloving etc.

As a result, your earthly father could affect how you see your heavenly Father. No questions asked, your heavenly Father loves you. He wants you to reverence than fear him. Do you see reverence as respect? For instance, there are some things you will not do in your parent's home, out of respect. As an adult, folk usually don't fear their parents; they respect them. And it's remarkably the same with God. He wants you to respect who he is in your life. He's amazingly more than another person in your life. As good as gold, he is your all in all. Everything about your life starts and ends with him.

Accordingly, the key to having an effective prayer life and suddenly knowing how to pray is connected to how well you understand who you're praying to. You think this is simple, I'm praying to God our Father. Ah, but do you understand who God our Father is?

Let's go back to the drawing board like in elementary school—you know a sentence like: "God is _____." The sentence becomes challenging because he is so much more; it's impossible to start a limited sentence and do justice to God. For this reason, is your mindset secure in understanding what and who you're calling upon at the beginning of your prayer when you say 'Our Father'? Use of the word "our" instead of "my" shows unselfish prayer.

Thus, you're also reminded that you're a part of his family. Others are your brothers and sisters in Christ as well as the world, because he is their Father too. You can bet your bottom dollar, he wants to be a part of everyone's life. Beyond belief, he is not a dead-beat dad or a father not wanting to have a special, meaningful relationship with his children. And you treat all others like family members. Additionally, the word 'Father' teaches that you pray to him [the Father].

First, let's cover God's omnipotence (his power, which means ALL power). In essence, all power belongs to him. He startlingly created the world. The first chapter of Genesis tells of its amazing happening. He suddenly spoke the world into being. The Book of Psalm tells us to look around and marvel at his new creations (Psalm 8). Become an insider and take a minute to look at the stars, he did it. Look around and see the sun and the moon. He did it.

Imagine how large and deep the oceans are—God's miracle doing. Come along and think about how he remarkably separated the darkness to make day and night—sensational! Don't forget all the living things too—introducing the plants and animals. And don't forget the most important thing of all, man. He quickly and easily created man; he created you (Psalm 139:13-18).

Be one of the few and get into your head, soul and heart his ironclad power. I'm sure there are many, many more things that can attest to his great power. Yes sir! This is who you're praying to. Extraordinarily, he created the world in 6 days; but truly it'll blow your mind that he could have done it in 1 day. Why? Be the first to hear he did it to teach us about order. As you look at Genesis, each day and the things created in each day build on each other. Therefore, it's vital that we make our prayer life orderly.

Second, let's move to God's omniscience or total knowledge. Psalm 139: 1-6 tells us how he is all knowing. And Jeremiah 1:4-5 also gives us insight on how well he knows us. Sometimes things (e.g., sins) in our past make us hesitant to go to him because we feel unworthy, shameful and guilty. Let me set your mind at ease; we are all unworthy. He knows this. Jesus died for us knowing we were unworthy.

So, let's go to God the way Hebrews 4:16 tells us—boldly (even though we have sinned) to the throne of grace to receive mercy and find grace to help you in your time of need. He knows everything, there are no secrets or surprises. It's all good that you have access to the Father. For instance, if you wanted something done in the city and had a difficult time getting it done, it may frustrate you. Yet, if you have a relationship with the city mayor, you have members only access to the mayor. A golden key can open any door.

As a result of you having quick access to the mayor, coupled with a special relationship, it is more than likely that you can suddenly bode well. You'll get your request done before everybody else. Access is the key. Too often, we don't exercise our access to the Father as often as we should. To have access to the Father, means no limits, no boundaries. Access him daily. The Bible tells us to pray morning, noon, and night. Hurry and use your access card today and visit the throne of grace.

Next, God is omnipresent. By and large, he is everywhere; the camera cannot lie. Psalm 139:7-12 asks where you can go to get away from his presence. You cannot go anywhere to get away from him. He tells the Israelites in Deuteronomy 4:31, he would not forsake them. He also will not forsake (i.e., desert or abandon) you.

You're an insider and first to get an idea about who God, our Father, is. He is love. Imagine love from your idea of a perfect earthly father. Now magnify your vision of love a million times—your heavenly Father's love. A love so perfect you could never achieve it from anyone else. The parable of the Lost Son (Luke 15:11-32) also instantly shows us the kind of loving father he is. Like a loving father, he listens to your prayers and always gives his best. Sometimes, this result may not always be exactly what you want—sometimes a loving parent even has to use the word "No" or "Not Now!"

When you have a child, the love of many parents for their child is so strong, they would die for them. They'll do anything in the world for their child. As a parent, could you carbon-copy and do as God did? Give them up for someone else, someone so undeserving, someone so ungrateful, someone who can be so mean-spirited and hateful and most of all someone so unloving? He sacrificed for us.

Jesus is his only son. Think about it, his only child. He gave him up. There was a time when Jesus was on the cross, God had to turn away from him. The time on the cross when Jesus took on our lifetime sins, he had to turn away since he could not be a part of sin. He was seen and heard. When this separation occurred, Jesus cried out, "My God, My God, why have you forsaken me?" Imagine the pain to be separated from his only child, even if it was only for a moment. Can you close your eyes and think of the pain of knowing that your child is in so much pain, and calling out to you without answer? Could you do the same thing?

How amazing it is that someone loves something so much they will pay full price (give their life) for damaged goods. He immediately paid cash on the nail for us. We are all damaged goods. Yet, Christ died for us. Would you pay full price for a damaged item at the store? Most likely, you wouldn't purchase the item, or you'd ask for a discounted price. See, no matter how you see yourself, God sees you as his child. As a parent, no matter what terrible thing your children do, you still love them. You see a glimmer of hope in them.

God did this because he loved us so much. He knew exactly the type of people we were and still are. He still loves you in spite of your ways. In Jeremiah 31:3, he tells us, "I have loved you with a love that lasts forever. I have kept on loving you with a kindness that never fails." His love is so perfect and unconditional; no one else comes close to giving us amazing love!

Don't have a clue and forgot who you were. But remember, you were adopted (i.e. (engrafted) by the Father. God chose us; he chose you. Before him, you were an orphan and fatherless. What a privilege that our Father adopted us despite our shortcomings, issues, and handicaps.

Regardless of how bad the relationship was or not having an earthly father, when praying "Father," you're blessed to have a father loving you more than you love yourself. God is such a good Father; you can call a spade a spade no father can come close. Also, now that you've been adopted, you have the right to all of the inheritance, riches and glory that Christ has. Like he obtained his glory by being obedient, you too must remember it's the obedient and trusting child instead of the rebellious and faithless child receiving the blessing. This is the Father you are to pray to. A reminder, he is also our provider and protector.

Let's bring it back to your earthy father. How do you feel when you disappoint him? Most folk don't feel good about it, right? Well, when you say "Our Father," think of all the things you've done today to please him. And now focus on the things you've done to not please him today. Daddy's girl or daddy's favorite son? Did daddy smile and say well done son or daughter—"My girl, you can do it?" Or did daddy say, "Don't do it, you know better. I taught you better?" Is God always pleased with your relationships? Daddy-being omniscient knows everything.

So, when you pray, focus on God as your Father. Meditate on your charmed life relationship and set the atmosphere of being open and honest with your father. Ask yourself, what can you do to be a better child as well as obedient to the Father? Think on areas in your life in complete shambles and where you're not living to the standards of your Father. Pray about those things. Knowing him as your Father means you have access to him and he will personally take care of you. The first part of prayer is the establishment of the right relationship with the Father. Remember, all he wants is you as a chip off the old block to reverence him.

Chapter 2

Who Art in Heaven

Y OU SHOULD NOT THINK of God being in a faraway place, because God is everywhere. He is right there. Acts 17:27-28 reminds us "...he is not far from any of us." For in him we live and move and have our being..."This petition of the prayer reminds you to acknowledge his sovereignty over the prayer; it also distinguishes the one, true God in heaven from all the false ones worshiped by man on earth. Heaven, the Father's house, is the true homeland.

Heaven is a real place. The Bible speaks of heaven's existence—and access to heaven through faith in Jesus Christ—but there are no petitions giving us a MapQuest-style location. *Heaven is where God is.* He is always near you when you call on him (James 4:8), and you're encouraged to "draw near" to him (Hebrews 10:1, 22).

The Bible says God in heaven is always near to his children on earth. Our Father who is in heaven wants us to focus on heavenly things. During prayer and meditation time, focus on heaven. Avoid focusing your minds on earth and what you have to get done. Focus on heaven. Heaven is where you want to go; heaven is a place of peace, joy, happiness, love, and all glory. Ask yourself during prayer, did you let heaven down today? Did you glorify heaven today? Did you fly heaven's banner today by telling others about heaven?

See, the enemy does not want you to talk about heaven. Hell or high water, he wants to keep you in the dumps. He desires you keep quiet so that the world can think there is no heaven, nor hell. As a result, you may feel your heavenly Father isn't loving. During this prayer time, give the Devil his due and focus on things you can do to make heaven proud. As you think about heaven, are there loved ones, neighbors or co-workers you are not sure whether they are going to heaven if they died? Pray for them, but also pray that God uses you in a way to help them in receiving Christ.

Let's commit ourselves to magnifying heaven today. Oftentimes, folk don't want to talk about heaven because it infers that one has to die or have one foot in the grave. But the Bible tells us to "Think about things that are in heaven. Don't think about things that are only on earth." (Colossians 3:2). So, during prayer, to keep your prayer orderly before the King, set your minds on heaven—permanent things and not temporary things.

Many people come in on a wing and a prayer and focus too much on things not lasting. As a follower, you're renting time here on earth; it's not your permanent place. Therefore, as renters, shun getting comfortable and realize that you're only here a short-time. People's lives are going down the tubes and folk are dropping like flies. 2 Corinthians 4:18, says "So we don't spend all our time looking at what we can see. Instead, we look at what we can't see. That's because what can be seen lasts only a short time. But what can't be seen will last forever."

Chapter 3

Hallow Be Thy Name

'HALLOWED' MEANS 'HOLY'. KEEPING God's name holy means you should honor, respect and admire who he is and what he has done. "Hallowed be your name" is telling you to worship God and to praise him for who he is. Eat, drink and be merry; you should pray with worship to him because he is so worthy of it. So, as a review, when you pray: (1) focus on the father (2) focus on heaven and (3) focus on hallowing his name.

Israel reverenced God's name so much they would not even say his name. During prayer, now that we've created a heavenly atmosphere, it's also time to worship him like the heavenly angels and saints. Face the music and see prayer as more than communication. Prayer is not an event, prayer is an experience. Anytime, you can experience him and his presence, it's time to bow and worship him.

"Father, I praise you and I worship you. You are holy. I give you honor. I give you all the glory." Use your own words. God recognizes a sincere heart. He does not require pretty words, eloquent phrases, fancy language, or wordy, meaningless rituals. And you do not have to be so deep or sophisticated or use a wide vocabulary. Telling him what's in your heart with your own words counts a great deal to him. Keep it simple. You do not need to impress him.

Even though Israel had the glory of God overseeing them, they didn't act like they had his glory. Your praise everyday lets him know how much you love him are is satisfied with him as your Father. This petition 'Hallowed be your name' serves as a reminder to praise and worship him daily. However, many saints are excellent in praise and worship, but their lives don't glorify or adore the Father. Therefore, whatever you do, fight the good fight, and do it in his name. Philippians tells us that whatever you do, word of deed, do it in his name.

Publicly, by your walk (which is a marathon) and not a Sunday stroll, glorify the Father. If not, repent for the things not glorifying him or repent for the things you could've done better to glorify him—hallowed be his name. How wonderful and excellent is his name. Unfortunately for this world, the only Jesus unbelievers see is often in you.

God is no flash in the pan; our Father and his name is holy and hallowed. God has many names, each describing a different aspect of his multi-faceted character. His name isn't mud, and here are some of the better-known names of God in the Bible:

EL, ELOAH: God "mighty, strong, prominent" (Genesis 7:1; Isaiah 9:6) – *El* appears to mean "power," as in "I have the power to harm you" (Genesis 31:29). *El* is associated with other qualities, such as integrity (Numbers 23:19), jealousy (Deuteronomy 5:9), and compassion (Nehemiah 9:31), but the root idea of might remains.

ELOHIM: God "Creator, Mighty and Strong" (Genesis 17:7;

Jeremiah 31:33) – the plural form of *Eloah*, which accommodates the doctrine of the Trinity. From the Bible's first sentence, the matchless nature of his power is evident as God (Elohim) speaks the world into existence (Genesis 1:1).

EL SHADDAI: "God Almighty," "The Mighty One of Jacob"

(Genesis 49:24; Psalm 132:2, 5) – speaks to his ultimate power over all.

ADONAI: "LORD" (Genesis 15:2; Judges 6:15) – used in place of YHWH, which was thought by the Jews to be too sacred to be uttered by sinful men. In the Old Testament, YHWH is more often used in his dealings with his people, while *Adonai* is used more when he deals with the Gentiles.

YHWH, YAHWEH or JEHOVAH: "LORD" (Deuteronomy 6:4; Daniel 9:14) – strictly speaking, the only proper name for God. Translated in English Bibles "LORD" (all capitals) to distinguish it from *Adonai*, "LORD." The revelation of the name is first given to Moses "I Am who I Am" (Exodus 3:14). This name specifies an immediacy, a presence. Yahweh is present, accessible, near to those who call on Him for deliverance (Psalm 107:13), forgiveness (Psalm 25:11) and guidance (Psalm 31:3).

YAHWEH-JIREH: "The LORD Will Provide" (Genesis 22:14) – the name memorialized by Abraham when God provided the ram to be sacrificed in place of Isaac.

YAHWEH-RAPHA: "The LORD Who Heals" (Exodus 15:26) – "I am Jehovah who heals you" both in body and soul. In body, by preserving from and curing diseases, and in soul, by pardoning iniquities.

YAHWEH-NISSI: "The LORD Our Banner" (Exodus 17:15), where *banner* is understood to be a rallying place. This name commemorates the desert victory over the Amalekites in Exodus 17.

YAHWEH-M'KADDESH: "The LORD Who Sanctifies, Makes

Holy" (Leviticus 20:8; Ezekiel 37:28) – God makes it clear that he alone, not the law, can cleanse his people and make them holy.

YAHWEH-SHALOM: "The LORD Our Peace" (Judges 6:24) – the name given by Gideon to the altar he built after the Angel of the LORD assured him he would not die as he thought he would after seeing him.

YAHWEH-ELOHIM: "LORD God" (Genesis 2:4; Psalm 59:5) – a combination of God's unique name YHWH and the generic "LORD," signifying he is the LORD of LORDs.

YAHWEH-TSIDKENU: "The LORD Our Righteousness" (Jeremiah 33:16) – It is God alone who provides righteousness to man, ultimately in the person of his Son, Jesus Christ, who became sin for us so that "we might become the Righteousness of God in him" (2 Corinthians 5:21).

YAHWEH-ROHI: "The LORD Our Shepherd" (Psalm 23:1) – After David pondered his relationship as a shepherd to his sheep, he realized God had the exact relationship with him, and so he declares, "Yahweh-Rohi is my Shepherd. I shall not want" (Psalm 23:1).

YAHWEH-SHAMMAH: "The LORD Is There" (Ezekiel 48:35) –

The name ascribed to Jerusalem and the Temple there, indicating the once-departed glory of the LORD (Ezekiel 8—11) had returned (Ezekiel 44:1-4).

YAHWEH-SABAOTH: "The LORD of Hosts" (Isaiah 1:24; Psalm 46:7) – *Hosts* means "hordes," both of angels and of men. He is LORD of the host of heaven and of the inhabitants of the earth, of Jews and Gentiles, of rich and poor, master and slave. Expressive of the majesty, power, and authority of God, he is able to accomplish what he determines to do.

EL ELYON: "Most High" (Deuteronomy 26:19) – derived from the Hebrew root for "go up" or "ascend," for which the implication is the highest. *El Elyon* denotes exaltation and speaks of absolute right to Lordship.

EL ROI: "God of Seeing" (Genesis 16:13) – the name ascribed to God by Hagar, alone and desperate in the wilderness after being driven out by Sarah (Genesis 16:1-14). She also realized *El Roi* saw her in her distress and testified he is a God who lives and sees all.

EL-OLAM: "Everlasting God" (Psalm 90:1-3) – God's nature is without beginning or end, free from all constraints of time, and he contains within himself the cause of time itself. "From everlasting to everlasting, you are God."

EL-GIBHOR: "Mighty God" (Isaiah 9:6) – the name describing the Messiah, Christ Jesus, in this forewarned is forearmed portion of Isaiah. As a powerful and mighty warrior, the Messiah, the Mighty God, will accomplish the destruction of his enemies and rule with a rod of iron (Revelation 19:15).

As you can see, it's a foregone conclusion that our Father has many names. For good measure, getting to know him personally tells you what name to use. An example, a guy was the head coach on his son's softball team. His son of flesh and blood normally calls him dad, but he immediately remembers to call him "coach." Even though the son was right about his dad, in the capacity at the softball game, he is operating as a coach first, and dad second. And the coach didn't fly off the handle. His son knew the difference because he knew his dad well. However, often times you may use a general term and say "God" instead of being more personal and referring to the name you want to revere The Father. If you're praying for the Father to provide something for you, flat out say "Jehovah Jireh." If praying for The Father to heal you, "Jehovah Rapha" fits to a tee. To many, this is a small thing, but you can call upon his name in the capacity he's operating in.

Chapter 4

Thy Kingdom Come

GOD IS KING, so he has a kingdom. His kingdom is the sign of what Jesus did on the cross and why he did it. Jesus died so we no longer bind ourselves by sin—happy as a lark. Then, justice and peace will reign in the world. Sin could be wiped out—hasta la vista, baby! We are to pray his kingdom will come—Jesus will come back and make it so. The kingdom will come in glory when Christ hands it over to his Father. You can also pray for the growth of his kingdom in your life today.

God is a fair, loving king. By saying "thy kingdom come," you are saying "Be my king." So, you're asking hard and fast for help in order to act, talk, and think the way God wants you to. You're petitioning to guide you today in showing you how you can uplift his kingdom. You know he wants the earth to be as his kingdom. What can you do today to bring glory to his kingdom? Ask to be used as his witness.

Since you realize our Father is a King, you must be a prince or princess. Therefore, meditate on being an ambassador for Christ, representing your kingdom nation—heaven. (2 Corinthians 5:20).

Let's talk about being a hoity-toity ambassador. He calls you to be an ambassador, like a United States Ambassador, so it's high time you must be a good citizen first.

The President of the U.S. will not pick a person having a history of illegal incidents to be an Ambassador. Most times, before one can be a high and mighty ambassador, they must go through the scrutiny of personal background checks or extreme vetting to ensure they're competent and credible to represent the U.S. Our King doesn't hold your past against you—Thank God! However, because he doesn't hold your past against you, you don't have a license to sin or live below his standards. Because of his grace, you can show your appreciation of it by not abusing it.

Even though, God calls you as a heavenly ambassador, are you a good citizen of heaven? If good citizenship is needed to represent the U.S., it's horse sense that you can envision your Christian goal as a good citizen representing heaven. During this time of meditation about the kingdom, meditate on your hot-off-the-press responsibilities as an ambassador. If the world saw you, can they tell you are from another nation, or do you act like the world?

Often, like identity theft, you can tell someone is from another country by the way they talk, dress or behave. When you open your mouth, do you talk like you are from heaven? When you dress, do you dress like you are from heaven or have you blended into this world? Can anyone tell you are not from this world? If you have short-comings in this area, meditate on areas you need to improve.

Beware the Ides of March, many unsaved folk will not come to know Jesus because they have been poor examples and ambassadors of what Christianity is all about. Have you caused anyone to stumble because of your lack of talk about heaven, or that your behavior was not Christ-like?

Chapter 5

Thy Will Be Done

FOR ALL INTENTS AND purposes, you are praying for the advancement of God's kingdom and remembering your role to carry out in this petition of the Lord's Prayer. Asking for his kingdom and for his will to be done is surrendering to him. His rule and his plans are the best things for your life—his will, his way, your faith. It's not rocket science, you are to pray for his plan in your life and in the world, not your own plan. If the shoe fits, pray for his will to be done versus your own. In heaven everyone submits to him. There is no selfishness, no cruelty, no lies—but plenty of love, peace and happiness.

You are to pray for what God wants instead of what you want. Did you know he has a specific will for your life? Part of connecting with him is saying, "God, what is your will for me today? I want to do your will." His will is forgetting about your wants, desires and needs—only concentrating on what will please our Father. And he wants earth to be like or as close to heaven as possible. All the good things in heaven can be here on the ends of the earth according to his will. We've all read or heard about what a wonderful place heaven is. No more dying, no sicknesses or diseases, no sin or conflict—enjoying being with and praising our heavenly Father.

Pray his will: "Father I want what you want. Because you are God, what I want doesn't matter if it's not your will." Look at Psalm 143:10. David asks God to teach him to do God's will. Jesus prayed in the Garden of Gethsemane that his will be done, not Jesus.

Do you know God's will for your life? This is an opportunity for you to get to ask him to show you his will for your life. However, many of us have asked him and haven't discovered our will. Time and again, we are looking for some great work to do to fully understand our will. Whatever you love doing is his will for your life. So, whatever it is, you must seek him to align your will in sync with his plan for your life. He created all of us and he made all of us different. Therefore, he has a specific calling designed for all of us. It matches our genetic makeup.

But too often, since you don't know what your will is, you may get involved in a lot of things that the Father didn't tell you to get involved in. Therefore, pray and ask him his will for you. If you know his will for your life, pray that he helps you stay in his will. Also, when it seems that he is taking you on a journey or in another direction, pray that he reveal his will if the cap fits. Pray you also remain patient and disciplined while he takes you to the next station of life on your journey.

It is vital that you become unselfish and allow God to do his will in your life, and assist him in doing it on earth. Strive not only as a fan of the kingdom, but also as a true participant. Stay thankful he is God, for he knows the plans of your life. "I know the plans I have for you," announces the Lord. "I want you to enjoy success. I do not plan to harm you. I will give you hope for the years to come." (Jeremiah 29:11).

Part 2

Sustaining Your Needs

Chapter 6

Give Us Today Our Daily Bread

S O PRAYER IS NOT only for God's heavenly glory, but is provided for our earthly good. He is not only interested in your spiritual life, but in your physical and material life as well. Now, it may not seem all spiritual to ask him for "bread," but you must keep in mind that his meaning here addresses not physical bread, but also "bread" of the spiritual sort.

When you pray, "Give us this day our daily bread," you are expressing your dependence on God and conveying your gratitude for his gracious provision in your life. "Daily bread" symbolizes the bread of life and everything you need for your life, for the day.

It is not demanding that he give you food, but reminding you not to take for granted everything you have. You agree he is the one who gives life and sustains you each day. Your cup runs over—you'll have more than enough for your needs.

Man does not live by bread alone; we depend on God for daily physical and spiritual food. Praying for daily bread reminds you to live one day at a time. Lamentations tells us that his mercies are new every morning. Matthew 6:34 tells us "don't worry about tomorrow. Tomorrow will worry about itself. Each day has enough trouble of its own." You ask him to give you today your daily bread. You are to pray for one day at a time.

Remember the song, "'One day at a time Sweet Jesus." Father give us today our daily bread. Father today I need your provision, I need your grace. I need your protection. This day, I need you. If you pray every day, you are telling God that you need him always—his love, guidance, and forgiveness.

Father, your word says you have never seen the righteous forsaken nor its seed begging bread (Psalm 37:25). Righteousness is not a state of being dressed a certain way, talking a certain way, or being so holy; you can't touch anything. Abraham was counted righteous by God because of his faithfulness. Abraham believed him. Abraham wasn't perfect. As you recall in Genesis, he lied to King Pharaoh about the status of his wife, Sarah. Noah was also counted righteous because he believed him.

Please don't take God's provision for granted. He has given us jobs; yet we complain. He has given us good health; yet we complain. He has given us a home; yet we complain. He has given us clothes; yet we complain. Truly, no matter how hard you work, how much you earn, and how cleverly you invest, save and buy in market forces, all you have is a gift from his hand. Every good thing and many happy returns come from him.

What is your greatest need today? Bring it to God in prayer. The Book of Psalm tells us the LORD is my shepherd I should not want—which means I should not be in want of anything. He will provide. Psalm 100 tells us we are the sheep of his pasture. Therefore, as the Shepherd, he is obligated to see that his "trusting and faithful" sheep are fed, sheltered and protected.

Chapter 7

Forgive Us Our Debts, As We Also Have Forgiven Our Debtors

WE NEED TO ASK God to forgive us of our sins—all the wrong things we have done, including our actions, thoughts and what we have said. Let's not mince words. You have to be sincere in saying my bad or sorry to him, and you must forgive others too. You should not keep something like being hurt by someone else a secret. Instead tell him, and after you talk about it, he will help you forgive those who hurt you. Jesus teaches that if you don't forgive others, God will not forgive you. What are our debts? We know a debt is something owed to another. What do we owe the Father? Simply, we owe him everything. What are our debts? In this case our debts are the multitude of sins we commit. We all commit sin and Jesus died such a horrific death on the cross because of our sins.

Matthew 6:14-15 states, "Forgive other people when they sin against you. If you do, your Father who is in heaven will also forgive you. But if you do not forgive the sins of other people, your Father will not forgive your sins." Ask Jesus to forgive you for your sins as he forgive others who sin against you. You don't have a right to hold forgiveness from others. In some cases it is difficult to forgive, as some people have done horrible things to us.

This is where Jesus comes in to help us. Ask him to help you forgive. Most of all, unforgiveness keeps you from having a full relationship with Jesus. It causes bitterness in you. It can make you physically ill. It can cause you to have anger in your heart and interfere in your relationship with others. All of those things can keep you from fully enjoying your life.

When you forgive others, you are not telling them that the sin committed against you is okay. Jesus is not telling us our sin is okay. What he is telling you is he will not hold your sin against you, and you should nip in the bud and not hold sin against each other.

In Jeremiah 31:34, Jesus told the Israelites he would not remember their sins: "I will forgive their evil ways. I will not remember their sins anymore." He will do the same for you with his forgiveness if you ask.

Also, Luke 23:32-34 shows: Two other men were also led out with Jesus to be killed. Both of them had broken the law. The soldiers brought them to the place called the Skull. There they nailed Jesus to the cross. He hung between the two criminals. One was on his right and one was on his left. Jesus said, "Father, forgive them. They don't know what they are doing." The soldiers divided up his clothes by casting lots.

Additionally, Stephen asked Jesus to forgive the people who were stoning him to death (Acts 7:59-61): While the members of the Sanhedrin were throwing stones at Stephen, he prayed. "Lord Jesus, receive my spirit," he said. Then he fell on his knees. He cried out, "LORD! Don't hold this sin against them!" When he had said this, he died.

If Jesus and Stephen could forgive the people for killing them, the heart of the matter is you can forgive others for sinning against you. Surely if Jesus, while dying a horrific death, could find it in his heart to forgive the people killing him, then you can forgive others for what they've done to you.

Reciting this scripture in The LORD's Prayer serves as a reminder for you to forgive those who have offended you. Do you forgive them? Think about those people you may not like. Do you forgive them? Are you praying for them?

It's critical you forgive them so the Father can forgive you. The fact of the matter is that many of the people who you don't forgive don't even know you're holding a grudge. When you forgive, it feels like the thing holding you back has been released. Also, while meditating, don't forget to confess your sins before God (1 John 1:9). He is faithful and just to forgive you.

But as you ask God for forgiveness, focus on true repentance and not true repeat. Unless we truly repent, our motive for asking for forgiveness is because we are unhappy about sinning against the Father, but keep asking for the "grace" card (get out of jail free-card) to remove our sins. Remember, your prayer time with him is about relationship and not religion. Religion says that you recite and you don't have to mean it. Relationship says you are not reciting, but speaking to him from a sincere heart.

Chapter 8

And Lead Us Not Into Temptation, But Deliver Us from Evil

T HIS PETITION OF THE prayer asks God for protection so you will be able to stand against all the bad influences in the world and achieve victory over sin. Feelings of anger, fear or loneliness can make you want to break a rule or sense temptation. Pray and feed your faith so he can help you with your feelings. Breaking a rule hurts him and you. He still loves you. Pray that he helps you know the difference between right and wrong.

You may be out of sorts or have a hard time with this petition. You may find it difficult why you would need to ask Jesus not to lead you into temptation. Jesus would never lead you into or tempt you to sin. It's against his nature.

Psalm 19:13 declares, "keep me from the sins I want to commit. May they not be my master. Then I will be without blame. I will not be guilty of any great sin against your law." The NCV scripture puts it even simpler. It says *"Keep me from the sins of pride; don't let them rule me. Then I can be pure and innocent of the greatest of sins."* You're asking God to keep you away, guide you from, and protect you from sinning; deliver you from Satan's evil tricks and temptations.

To put this in context, you face a clear and present danger in your generation. Behind the scenes a battle is being fought for the hearts and lives of men, women and children across the planet. Forces of evil and good are on the warpath waging an invisible war, between God himself and a created being known as Satan.

As a believer, you are in this battle and you're in it to the end. You are not a tourist on a vacation in this world if you're following Jesus. You are on the side of angels and a soldier on a mission for him. And the only way to win this war is to be on the ball, preparing and praying. Jesus taught us to pray in order to overcome the temptation of the enemy. When you pray, you are protecting your faith, your future and your family. In these times, you must remember you are fighting a spiritual battle; you can only win with the spiritual weapons he provides. He has promised deliverance for his praying children.

We are all tempted by so many things. The Bible tells us that God will not let you be tempted beyond what you can bear. And when you are tempted, he will provide a way for you to escape or show you a way out. Some ways you're tempted include lying, cheating, fornication and adultery to name a few.

While praying, ask the Father to show you areas where your armor is weak. Was I tempted today? Father through your Spirit, show me where I was tempted. Did I find pleasure in a potential tempting situation? Remember, James 1:13 tells us, *"When a person is tempted, they shouldn't say, "God is tempting me." God can't be tempted by evil. And he doesn't tempt anyone."*

Temptation is serious because if you succumb to it, in the end it will destroy you. Don't put yourself in situations where you're tempted. Don't paddle your own canoe and trust your flesh, it will let you down, for the spirit is willing; but the flesh is weak. Ask God to show you—spiritually search you—and reveal all your temptations, even the hidden ones you try to suppress or keep others from knowing. Satan cannot stop you from doing anything for his glory, but he can throw temptation into your life to trip you.

Temptation is a prelude to sin. If you subtly preview the trailer, eventually you will become the main attraction in your sin-filled action movie. If you don't want temptation to follow you, don't act like you're interested. Satan couldn't stop Adam and Eve, but he used temptation to stop them from living a life of abundance. Is the same happening to you? Check yourself and find out your weak point. Is it the lust of the flesh? The lust of the eyes? Or the pride of life?

If you realize Satan is tempting you, you must strengthen yourself in these areas. Remember, temptation is a prelude to sin and evil. As a devil's advocate, don't do it—everything you've worked for can be lost in a minute. All good things comes to he who waits. In the end, to keep God's trust when you continually succumb to temptation:

Think on the things you're tempted of.

Did you come close to falling today?

Did you willingly allow temptation to be around you today?

Did you notice the escape/emergency exit door?

Sin promises to serve and please, and in the end it comes to rule and destroy. Has one bite of temptation put you into a spiraling effect on the road to destruction? Is temptation now an addiction?

Finally "But deliver us from evil" means God gave you a way to escape or he'll snatch you out of a tempting and potential situation. His Spirit will not force you to take an escape or exit; it's up to you. Pray that he will deliver you, for his spirit gives you victory over temptation. Sincerely ask yourself, do you want him to deliver you or do you want him to forgive you? Do you see the things tempting you as evil or pleasure?

Chapter 9

For Thine is The Kingdom and The Power And The Glory Forever

GOD IS THE REAL King. If you want to be part of his kingdom, you must trust him to teach you to pray, to understand the Bible, and to help you love others. He is almighty and deserves glory. It's all about you Father—your kingdom, your power and your glory forever, for all eternity. It's not about me. I exist because of you.

This petition of the prayer can remind you of your purpose in Life; it's not a pipe dream. You're prompted you exist for God's pleasure and not your own. It can ring a bell that in everything you go through, he has the power to overcome. When you truly believe you're walking in his will and purpose, you can have less concerns and more peace; you stress less and can experience happiness and joy in your life.

The words "thine is the kingdom" can continually remind you of God. You're encouraged to ask, "Father, show me areas in my life where I've put things ahead of you and your kingdom and don't give you glory." Did the words I say today give you glory? Did my actions give you glory? Did my thoughts give you glory? Do my new relationships give you glory? Do the roles you call me in as a saint give you glory? As your role as a wife, did I give you glory? As a husband, did I give you glory? As an employee on the job, did I give you glory? As a friend did I give you glory?'

Play it again Sam! This appeal also gives you the reassurance that you'll see heaven and prompt you to think on heavenly things. Scripture says to "set your heart and mind on the things above." Hurricane Katrina gave us a daily reminder of what things are important. You can spend years storing up fine things on earth. However, you can lose it in a second, such as the hurricane victims did. Make your whole focus on where your position is in heaven.

Poetic justice is we're so rebellious that if God has to give us a passing grade for heaven, it'll be a point-blank 'D.' Preposterous, and it wouldn't be an 'F,' because everyone passes if you accept Jesus Christ. Preaching to the choir, it wouldn't be a 'C,' because Romans 12:1 reminds us that it's our reasonable service we make our bodies a living sacrifice. Reasonable means it's average or ordinary; he is not asking you to do anything extraordinary or great...be average—reasonable.

When Israel was in the wilderness, even though the glory of the LORD was with them (cloud by day and fire by night), they did not truly glorify God. They were pressed into service about pleasing their flesh and not about having an awesome relationship with almighty God. Even though you pray for his glory? Are you like Israel? Are you rebellious? Are you stubborn? Are you a complainer? Do you feel like sometimes you made a mistake by establishing this relationship with him? Are you fearful of where he wants to take you?

Chapter 10

Amen

THE HEBREW WORD TRANSLATED "amen" means "truly," "so be it" or "I don't know when or how, but I know Jesus will answer my prayer." You may paraphrase as: "truth;" "so be it;" "Yes;" "I am confident;" "I accept it as truth;" "I believe it;" "Let it happen;" or "I can't wait!" In the Old Testament, "amen" is used by people answering to curses spoken by God on numerous evils (Deuteronomy 27:15-26). In the New Testament, the apostles—John, Paul, and Peter—utilized "amen" at the end of their letters. When Christians say "amen" at the end of prayers, we are following the model of the apostles, asking God to "please let it be as we have prayed." When you pray according to his will, you can be assured that he will answer "so be it" and grant your petitions (John 14:13; 1 John 5:14).

"Amen" says you agree with what God wants to do. You assent with the Father's response to your prayers instead of a tall story. You're in agreement that your prayer will change you for the better. We should not live without prayer; we must pray ceaselessly. You say yes prayer draws you closer to the Father. Subscribe you are victorious. You are of the same mind; you are blessed and he will continue to be your provider, protector, guide, comforter, etc.

Conclusion

Pray and Convey His Blessings for Others

Y OU CAN BET THE farm peoples' number one poll response of what they want most from prayer now would be "answers." When you pray, you're seeking an immediate response from God. In agreement with my *LORD Teach Me How to Pray* co-authors, Rodney Perry and Diane Smith, we believe that the most important lesson learned regarding prayer is that it is far better to be an answer to prayer than to get an answer to prayer. Why? Because he wants to answer prayers through us, according to his miracle power at work within us.

When you pray for others you allow yourself to be a new channel of blessing. God has remarkably blessed you, and through you, he can amazingly bless others. Luke 12:48 reminds us, "Much will be required of everyone who has been given much. Even more will be asked of the person who is supposed to take care of much."

The Bible is filled with tested examples of God using willing servants to convey his powerful blessings to others. Remember

Moses? Out there in the desert, he was praying for the children of Israel as the Israelites were praying in Egypt. And God came to Moses through a burning bush and said, "I have heard their cry." He told Moses he was going to be used by him to answer the prayer of the Israelites.

The Bible also names specific groups of people for whom you are to pray.

Public leadership. This includes the President and Congress, our national leaders, our state and local government leaders, police officers, teachers, and others in authority. Whether or not you agree with their policies and opinions, you are to pray that they would suddenly come to saving faith in Jesus Christ.

Spiritual Leaders. The devil aims his biggest guns at God's leaders, and today, many are discouraged, hurting, and even falling into sin. His people need to pray for his leaders. Pray now for the pastors, missionaries, and Christian leaders in America and throughout the world.

Our Country. We need to cry out to God and pray for our country. And if you love this country you will pray for him to revive his Church. Pray that he would renew families and communities. Pray for your fellow citizens and neighbors, and turn your prayers to action. Psalm 33:12 says, "Blessed is the nation whose God is the Lord. Blessed are the people he chose to be his own." Join in prayer that our nation will return to its roots of honoring God today.

The Lost. Are you praying for those in your life who do not know Jesus? Prayer is the ultimate means by which you help point others to faith in Christ. You and I know people who have yet to receive God's gift of grace, and the first step you can instantly take is to commit the matter to prayer. Only he, by his Spirit, can reach a neighbor, rescue a reckless child, and turn a strong-willed heart toward him.

While it is wonderful to pray, "LORD, help missionaries?" God's response may be, "Now I want you to go and share the Good News!" If you're praying, "LORD, save lost people," listen carefully because he may put your hot feet to your prayers and say, "You go and tell your friend about me." Are you willing to be a big answer to prayer?

As you pray 'The LORD's Prayer' today, open *LORD Teach Me How to Pray* and take time to soak in the proven meaning of each line. First, ask God to show you a specific way in which you can bless someone today. Keep the eyes of your heart open for opportunities he will place in your heart. Pray specifically for his complete will to be done on earth as it is in heaven.

Now, you've read this book, we pray that you have increased your prayer life. Thus, you have put yourself on the road to spiritual prosperity which will manifest to material wealth and life success. Jesus continually prayed and we know the results. Every knee shall bow and every tongue shall confess that he's LORD. All because he understands prayer and the effects of prayer. Matthew 6:9 was the essence of his ministry. As a final word, everything starts with prayer.

Appendix A

Prerequisite For Prayer

To HELP US BE more Christ-like and live a life of holiness and have answered prayers, we must first make sure we are fulfilling the prerequisites to proper prayer.

Purity of heart. – Purity of hearts means we should be simple, clear, genuine, real, and true when we come to God in whatever capacity, especially in prayer. Matthew 5:8, NIV says, "*Blessed are the pure in heart, for they will see God.*" Not only will you see God, but you are also able to communicate, talk and pray to and with Him.

Psalm 66:18-19 TLB tells us, "*If I had not confessed sin in my heart, my Lord would not have listened. But God did listen! He paid attention to my prayer.*" Psalm 66:18-19 ICV says, "*If I had known of any sin in my heart, the Lord would not have listened to me. But God has listened. He has heard my prayer.*" These petitions in Psalm above do mean we cannot have sinned. Paul in Romans tells us that **all** have sinned and come short of the glory of God. Psalm 66:18 means the heart must be right. If we have sin in our heart, we need to confess it.

Believe – Matthew 21:22 NIV says, "If *you believe, you will receive whatever you ask for in prayer.*" Hebrews 11:6b TLB tells us, "*Anyone who wants to come to him must believe that there is a God and that he rewards those who sincerely seek him.*

You must have enough faith to believe God is who He says He is and will answer your prayer. Your prayers will be answered; however, they will not always be answered in the way that you desire. This is where you begin trusting God to have your best interest at heart and will always do what is best for you.

In Christ's Name – John 14:13, NIV says, "*And I will do whatever you ask in my name, so that the Son may bring glory to the Father.* "You do this because you must believe Jesus is the Son of God and He died for our sins. Unless you have acknowledged Jesus as God's Son and a part of the Trinity—Father, Son, Holy Spirit, you cannot have a relationship with Him.

Isaiah 53:4-6 TLB gives us an excellent example of what Jesus did for us. The scripture puts it this way: "*Yet it was our weaknesses he carried; it was our sorrows that weighed him down. And we thought his troubles were a punishment from God for his own sins! But he was wounded and crushed for our sins. He was beaten that we might have peace. He was whipped, and we were healed! All of us have strayed away like sheep. We have left God's paths to follow our own. Yet the Lord laid on him the guilt and sins of us all.*"

According to God's Will – 1 John 5:14 (Amplified Bible) says, "*14And this is the confidence (the assurance, the privilege of boldness) which we have in Him: [we are sure] that if we ask anything (make any request) according to His will (in agreement with His own plan), He listens to and hears us.*"

1 John 5:14, NLT also tells us: "*14And we can be confident that he will listen to us whenever we ask him for anything in line with his will.*" Additionally, 1 John 5:14, NIRV says, "*14There is one thing we can be sure of when we come to God in prayer. If we ask anything in keeping with what he wants, he hears us.*"

Praying for God's will it's not easy to do. This takes total trust in God. You are saying it is not what I want Father, it's what your will is. What you want and his will do not always agree. You can be sure God's will is always the best for you.

Appendix B

10 Motivations
Why We Should Pray

E PHESIANS 2:18 NCV SAYS, "*Yes, through Christ we all have the right to come to the Father in one Spirit.*" Notice the scripture says, 'we all have the right.' We can come to him twenty-four hours a day seven days a week at no charge. It's free to seek the Lord. There are an abundant of reasons to pray and 10 motivations why we should pray follow:

1. *God's Word Calls Us to Pray* (Matthew 5:44; Matthew 6:5; Matthew 6:9; Romans 12:12; Ephesians 6:18; Philippians 4:6; Colossians 4:2; 1 Thessalonians 5:17; – 1 Timothy 2:1)

2. *Jesus Prayed Regularly* (Matthew 14:23; Matthew 26:36; Mark 1:35; Luke 5:16; Luke 6:12; Luke 18:1)

3. *Prayer is How We Communicate with God* (2 Chronicles 7:14; Isaiah 40:29-31; Hebrews 4:15-16)

4. *Prayer allows us to participate in God's Works*

5. ***Prayer gives us Power over Evil*** (Ephesians 6:12); 1 Timothy 4:8;) – Matthew 26:41

6. ***Prayer is Always Available*** (Psalm 139:7; Romans 8:38-39).

7. ***Prayer keeps us Humble before God*** (Proverbs 11:2; 22:4; Micah 6:8; Ephesians 4:2; James 4:10; Matthew 18:4)

8. ***Prayer Grants us the Privilege of Experiencing God***

9. ***Answered Prayer is a Potential Witness***

10. ***Prayer Strengthens the Bonds between Believers***

Appendix C

Some Reasons Why We Don't Pray

1. **We rather seek advice from others.** Sometimes instead of going to God who made us for answers, you may feel it's easier to just ask family or friends, who are not all-knowing, all-powerful, or all-present. We know sometimes when looking for a quick response, it's so convenient to ask others. Yes, that guidance may sound good and mean well, but it's best to hear it from God yourself.

2. **We don't know God.** A lot of people know of God, but do not truly know God. You may know a lot of people in life, but that's does not mean you know them. To know them means to truly know them. To know God, you must establish a relationship and truly be intimate with Him.

3. **We don't think we have time to pray:** One of the biggest tricks of the enemy is to convince you that you don't have time to pray; it's unimportant. The best way to defeat this adversary is through prayer instead of trying to fix it with our flesh. That's why we don't have time to pray because we waste time in our flesh.

4. **We don't think it is important; we don't understand the importance of prayer.** Again, Satan wants you to believe it's all a twist of fate. If you believe that, then you will have no reason to pray. If things just happen by chance or luck, then there is no reason to have faith there is a God nor listen to God. You're encouraged to fix your mind you cannot exist without prayer. Prayer is just as important as having air to breathe, food to eat, water to drink, a house to live in, and clothes for shelter.

5. **We don't believe God answers our prayers.** Just because God may not have answered your prayer or did not give you the response, you're petitioning for does not mean God does not answer prayer. If you have been praying for something for a long time and you have not received an answer, we suggest you ask again. See Appendix D.

6. **We don't know where to begin**: To be honest, many of us were never taught how to pray. Thus, we're glad you're reading *Lord Teach Us How to Pray*. You no longer must imitate others you've seen pray. Unless one understands prayer, we know it can be challenging to know where to begin or how to become an effective prayer warrior. Thus, we're so glad you're reading and receiving from *Lord Teach Us How to Pray*.

Appendix D

Some Explanations Why Prayers Go Unanswered

O NE OF THE GREATEST benefits afforded to every Christian is the privilege of answered prayers. In the Bible, Jesus made this tremendous promise, *"And whatever things you ask in prayer, believing, you will receive"* (Matthew 21:22). However, despite the Lord's willingness to answer prayer, it is obvious some prayers have gone unanswered. Why is this? The following are the most common reasons why some prayers do not get results:

1. **Lack of Fellowship with God and His word** (John 15:7)
2. **Not seeking to please the Lord** (1 John 3:22)
3. **Unconfessed Sin in One's Life** (1 Peter 3:12)
4. **Improper Motives** (James 4:3)
5. **Not asking in God's will** (1 John 5:14-15)
6. **Don't know how to pray** (Luke 11:1)
7. **Lack of Faith** (Hebrews 11:6)

Other Books
by Mark C. Overton

Win at Work

Faith Series

Faith Excellence
Faith Transformation

The Good Book Series

New Day, New Life
What Love Really Means
I Like to Start with Something Funny
Lord Teach Me How to Pray
Chapter and Verse

Airmen Series

Career Progression Guide for Airmen: The Basics
Career Progression Guide for Airmen

CPSIA information can be obtained
at www.ICGtesting.com
Printed in the USA
BVHW040524090623
665636BV00005B/283